Sir Walter Raleigh

English Explorer and Author

Colonial Leaders

Lord Baltimore
English Politician and Colonist

Benjamin Banneker
American Mathematician and Astronomer

Sir William Berkeley
Governor of Virginia

William Bradford
Governor of Plymouth Colony

Jonathan Edwards
Colonial Religious Leader

Benjamin Franklin
American Statesman, Scientist, and Writer

Anne Hutchinson
Religious Leader

Cotton Mather
Author, Clergyman, and Scholar

Increase Mather
Clergyman and Scholar

James Oglethorpe
Humanitarian and Soldier

William Penn
Founder of Democracy

Sir Walter Raleigh
English Explorer and Author

Caesar Rodney
American Patriot

John Smith
English Explorer and Colonist

Miles Standish
Plymouth Colony Leader

Peter Stuyvesant
Dutch Military Leader

George Whitefield
Clergyman and Scholar

Roger Williams
Founder of Rhode Island

John Winthrop
Politician and Statesman

John Peter Zenger
Free Press Advocate

Revolutionary War Leaders

John Adams
Second U.S. President

Ethan Allen
Revolutionary Hero

Benedict Arnold
Traitor to the Cause

King George III
English Monarch

Nathanael Greene
Military Leader

Nathan Hale
Revolutionary Hero

Alexander Hamilton
First U.S. Secretary of the Treasury

John Hancock
President of the Continental Congress

Patrick Henry
American Statesman and Speaker

John Jay
First Chief Justice of the Supreme Court

Thomas Jefferson
Author of the Declaration of Independence

John Paul Jones
Father of the U.S. Navy

Lafayette
French Freedom Fighter

James Madison
Father of the Constitution

Francis Marion
The Swamp Fox

James Monroe
American Statesman

Thomas Paine
Political Writer

Paul Revere
American Patriot

Betsy Ross
American Patriot

George Washington
First U.S. President

Famous Figures of the Civil War Era

Jefferson Davis
Confederate President

Frederick Douglass
Abolitionist and Author

Ulysses S. Grant
Military Leader and President

Stonewall Jackson
Confederate General

Robert E. Lee
Confederate General

Abraham Lincoln
Civil War President

William Sherman
Union General

Harriet Beecher Stowe
Author of Uncle Tom's Cabin

Sojourner Truth
Abolitionist, Suffragist, and Preacher

Harriet Tubman
Leader of the Underground Railroad

Sir Walter Raleigh

English Explorer and Author

Susan Korman

Arthur M. Schlesinger, jr.
Senior Consulting Editor

Chelsea House Publishers

Philadelphia

Produced by Pre-Press Company, Inc., East Bridgewater, MA 02333

CHELSEA HOUSE PUBLISHERS
Editor in Chief Stephen Reginald
Production Manager Pamela Loos
Art Director Sara Davis
Director of Photography Judy L. Hasday
Managing Editor James D. Gallagher
Senior Production Editor J. Christopher Higgins

Staff for *SIR WALTER RALEIGH*
Project Editor Anne Hill
Associate Art Director Takeshi Takahashi
Series Design Keith Trego

The Chelsea House World Wide Web address is http://www.chelseahouse.com

First Printing
1 3 5 7 9 8 6 4 2

Library of Congress Cataloging-in-Publication Data

Korman, Susan.
  Sir Walter Raleigh / Susan Korman.
    p. cm. — (Colonial leaders)
  Includes bibliographical references and index.
  ISBN 0-7910-5969-3 (HC); 0-7910-6126-4 (PB)
    1. Raleigh, Walter, Sir, 1552?–1618—Juvenile literature.
    2. Great Britain—Court and courtiers—Biography—Juvenile literature.
    3. Explorers—England—Biography—Juvenile literature. [1. Raleigh, Walter, Sir,
    1552?–1618. 2. Explorers.] I. Title. II. Series.
DA86.22.R2 K67 2000
942.05'5'092—dc21
  [B]
                                                              00-038379

Publisher's Note: In Colonial and Revolutionary War America, there were no standard rules for spelling, punctuation, capitalization, or grammar. Some of the quotations that appear in the Colonial Leaders and Revolutionary War Leaders series come from original documents and letters written during this time in history. Original quotations reflect writing inconsistencies of the period.

Contents

Walter Raleigh grew up on a farm called Hayes Barton in the county of Devon on the southwest coast of England. Walter spent his free time near the sea watching ships sail away and return. He enjoyed hearing the sailors' stories of their adventures in distant lands.

The Call
of the Sea

Walter Raleigh always felt a strong connection to the sea. He grew up in a small town in Devon, England, not far from the coast. As a boy he spent many hours on the rocky beach, watching seamen sail off to faraway lands. The sailors intrigued young Walter. Their stories about mysterious lands filled with gold and other treasures also shaped his vision of the future. Walter hoped that someday he, too, would set sail to explore the mysterious world across the ocean.

While Walter grew up near the water, his father was a country gentleman who farmed the land. The family's home, where Walter was born in either 1552 or 1554, was called Hayes Barton. It was a **cob-walled** farmhouse, which still stands today.

Walter had a brother named Carew and a sister named Margaret. The Raleigh children were expected to help their parents with the harvest. They also hunted rabbits and birds for the family's meals.

Walter's father, also named Walter Raleigh, had been married twice before. Walter's mother, Elizabeth, had also been married before. This provided Walter with a large family—and plenty of ready playmates. He most enjoyed the company of the Gilberts, his three half brothers on his mother's side: John, Humphrey, and Adrian. The boys were older than Walter and filled with active, adventurous spirits. Like Walter, Humphrey Gilbert dreamed about exploring the world.

The most common spelling of Walter's last name is *Raleigh*. However, Walter never used this version of his name. Instead he spelled it *Ralegh*. During his lifetime several other variations were used: *Rawley, Raulie, Rawleyghe,* and *Ralle.*

Sir Humphrey Gilbert's theories on the existence of a Northwest Passage between the Pacific and Atlantic Oceans helped to inspire Raleigh and other explorers.

Another family member who influenced Walter's early career was his cousin Gawain Champernowne. Gawain had married the daughter of a French nobleman, and he had gone to live in France to fight for the French Protestants known as the **Huguenots.** Walter was probably 14 years old when Gawain requested help from his friends and family back home. Walter, along with others, volunteered to cross the English Channel to help the Huguenot cause.

Walter's time on the battlefields of France made him grow up quickly. The cold-blooded killing he saw in France would always haunt him. When he returned to England, he was no longer an innocent lad with a cheerful outlook on life. He is said to have told his friends: "One thing I have learned: Civil war is an evil from which good can seldom come."

There is some confusion about the sequence of events in Walter's early life. It is believed that he enrolled at Oxford University after returning from France. His name appears on the university

As a student at the Middle Temple, which is considered to be the finest of the four Inns of Court, Walter would have met many of London's most famous people.

ledgers in 1572. But Walter did not stay long enough at Oxford to earn a degree. He was only 12 months away from graduating when he moved to London. There he enrolled at Middle Temple, a university where lawyers were trained.

Walter had a brilliant mind. However, he didn't take his law studies very seriously. Instead he used the opportunity to learn about London and enjoy the city's nightlife. He had a quick temper and sometimes got involved in brawls or fights. One evening a young man in a tavern annoyed Walter by droning on and on about something. Walter demanded that he stop talking. When the man refused, Walter decided to shut his mouth for him—by sealing his beard to his mustache with wax!

Although Walter did receive some formal education, most of what he knew, he taught himself. His interests were broad and wide-ranging. He enjoyed science and mathematics and loved to argue politics with others.

William Shakespeare is the most famous writer of the Elizabethan Age.

He constantly read and wrote poetry. Later, he became one of England's best-known writers, publishing several best-selling books of poetry and essays.

But Walter's main interest was politics. More than anything, he wanted to attract the notice of Elizabeth I—the powerful queen who reigned over England at the time. Once again Walter's family would play an important role in shaping the path of his career.

As a young man, Walter was still close to his half-brother, Humphrey Gilbert. Humphrey had approached the queen several times about settling a large **colony**

Queen Elizabeth I was one of England's greatest monarchs. She ruled from 1558 until her death in 1603. Her father was Henry VIII and her mother was Anne Boleyn. Since Elizabeth never married, she was often called the "Virgin Queen."

Her reign is known as the Golden Age and the Elizabethan Age. It was a time of rapid scientific discovery and great sea exploration. Many brilliant writers, including William Shakespeare and Edmund Spenser, published poetry and plays during this time. Under Elizabeth, England's economy thrived and the Church of England became the main church of the country.

in the New World. He believed that such a colony would bring Elizabeth more wealth. It would also strengthen England against its powerful enemy, Spain. But so far, Elizabeth had refused to grant Humphrey's request.

Walter suspected that Humphrey was thinking too grandly. He shrewdly realized that cautious Elizabeth was worried about the expedition's cost and many risks. He suggested that Humphrey propose a more modest plan.

Walter was right. Humphrey next proposed bringing a smaller number of settlers to the New World. This time Queen Elizabeth gave her permission.

Walter eagerly joined the group of men who set out in 1578. He was sure that the adventure would make him rich and famous. Instead, the voyage seemed doomed from the start. First, harsh sea gales battered the ships and forced the men to seek a safe harbor. The next time the boats set out, a Spanish **fleet** approached. During the battle that followed, Walter was wounded. One ship went down with men still on board. Humphrey was discouraged and decided to head home.

But Walter wasn't ready to admit failure. As soon as his wounds healed, he set out with his single ship. But once again the rough sea made it impossible to continue. Faced with dwindling **provisions** and a ship full of weary men, he was forced to return home.

Walter arrived back on England's shores frustrated and disappointed. The expedition had been an expensive failure. Queen Elizabeth made Walter and Humphrey pay large fines. Walter was probably wondering how to win back the queen's favor when another opportunity arose. This time it was across the sea in Ireland.

English colonists had been living in Ireland for generations. The two countries had lived in peace until Elizabeth's father, Henry VIII, broke his ties with the pope in Rome.

The Irish were loyal Catholics who followed the pope. They protested England's break with

Rome by staging bloody rebellions. Spain and Italy were helping them by sending troops to Ireland. Queen Elizabeth had been forced to send more and more soldiers to defend her rule there.

Walter was very ambitious. He knew that an English gentleman could win fame by fighting against the wild and rebellious Irish. In 1580 he traveled across the Irish Sea to become captain of an **infantry** company.

In Ireland, Walter seemed to display a new side of his personality—a ruthless side. Perhaps it was his memories of the war in France that made him fight so fiercely. One thing is certain: any Irish rebel caught by Walter Raleigh quickly met his death.

While Walter acted brutally against the enemy, his own men thought he was brave and smart. But it wasn't his fighting style that made Queen Elizabeth finally notice him. Instead, it was Walter's strong stand against one of his own countrymen, Lord Grey.

Lord Grey was governor of Ireland. Most people, including Walter, thought Lord Grey was a weak ruler. Walter's complaints about Lord Grey's policies in Ireland soon reached the queen's ears. Elizabeth wanted to hear more of this Captain Raleigh's opinions.

When Walter went to the court in 1581, he cut a dashing figure. Over six feet tall, he towered above most men. His brown hair was long and curly and his beard and mustache were finely groomed. He dressed in elegant clothing, with sparkling jewels on his fingers and a pearl in one ear. Everything about him radiated confidence and ambition.

Queen Elizabeth liked to surround herself with clever and attractive men. As Walter stood before her, he instantly impressed her with his wit and intelligence. After that, his rise was swift. Walter quickly became a favorite of the most powerful queen in England's history.

Queen Elizabeth I encouraged adven-
turers like Raleigh and Sir Francis
Drake to follow their dreams of
wealth and glory. Because they were
devoted to the queen, they were eager
to prove themselves to her.

A Rising Star

The 1580s were a very important time in Walter's career. He spent much of his time at the queen's court. Elizabeth constantly sought out his opinion on matters, calling him her **"oracle"** and her "Water," perhaps revealing that she found him essential. She valued his mind and his precise way of speaking.

To show her affection, the queen showered Walter with gifts of money, jewels, and land. She also gave him a valuable wine **monopoly.** This meant that Walter received an income from every English wine merchant. In 1584 the queen bestowed upon

There are two famous stories about Walter's passionate devotion to Queen Elizabeth. These stories have been passed down for hundreds of years. However, no one is sure if they're really true.

One day the queen was out walking with a group of her courtiers. Spotting a mud puddle in her path, Walter removed his velvet cloak. Gallantly, he laid it down in the mud so Elizabeth wouldn't get her feet dirty.

Another time Walter supposedly used a diamond ring (or the diamond-studded hilt of a sword) to scratch a message for Elizabeth on a window pane. "Fain would I climb, yet I fear to fall."

him the highest honor of all: he was made a knight. Now Walter was known as Sir Walter Raleigh.

In return, Walter wrote poems in Elizabeth's honor. He praised her eyes and auburn red curls, delighting her with his clever way with words.

Walter enjoyed his new role as **courtier.** But he missed the excitement of his earlier days. He still longed to explore the world outside England. He was certain that his country could become richer and more powerful by settling colonies in the New World.

Meanwhile Walter's half-brother, Sir Humphrey Gil-

**Raleigh's gallantry towards Elizabeth
helped make him her favorite courtier,
but worked against him when she
found that she could not spare him to
go on expeditions to the New World.**

bert, was planning another voyage of exploration. Walter decided to use his new wealth to
help pay for Humphrey's expedition. He also
supplied a ship, the *Bark Raleigh,* and persuaded
the queen to support Humphrey.

The colonists brought back many new things from the New World. One of them was tobacco. The men had seen Indians smoking tobacco in clay pipes.

Walter Raleigh was one of the first Englishmen to try smoking. When one of his servants first saw smoke coming from Walter's nose and mouth, he panicked— and tossed a bucket of cold water on his master.

Walter enjoyed smoking and encouraged others to take it up. In this way he is credited (or blamed!) with spreading the habit throughout England.

Walter longed to accompany his half brother, but the queen refused to let him go. She said that Walter was too valuable to leave her court. (Later Elizabeth would tell Walter that she had saved his life by saying no.)

Elizabeth was probably right. Once again Humphrey Gilbert hit hard luck. Illness, then violent storms, doomed the expedition. Finally, in September 1583, Humphrey and his ship, the *Squirrel,* were lost at sea.

Humphrey's death was an enormous loss for Walter. He missed his half brother terribly. But Humphrey's death also strengthened Walter's determination to explore the New World. He soon began making plans for another expedition.

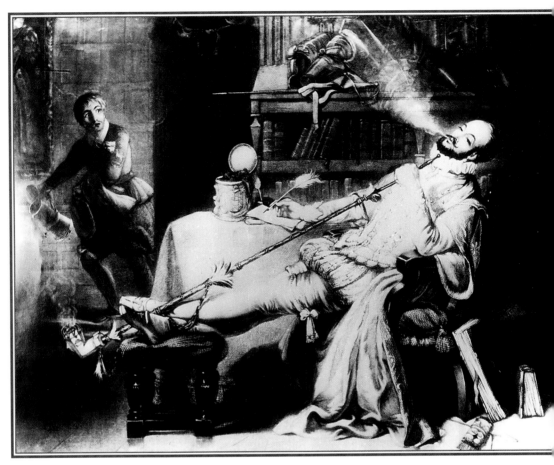

When one of Walter Raleigh's servants first saw him smoking, he panicked and rushed to throw water over him because he thought Walter was on fire.

Once again, Walter spent a lot of his own money on ships and supplies. He prepared the route carefully and recruited many smart and talented men. But once again Queen Elizabeth forbade him to accompany the explorers.

On April 27, 1584, two ships left Plymouth Harbor in England. In July of that year, they landed on what is now part of the Carolinas in the United States.

When the men returned to the queen's court the following year, they were full of stories about the land across the Atlantic. They'd met friendly Indians and seen fertile soil for farming. They even brought two Indians back to England. Their names were Manteo and Wanchese.

Many of the men wanted to return to the Americas to start a settlement. With Walter's encouragement, the queen gave her permission. It was agreed that the name of the new colony would be "Virginia" after the "Virgin" Queen.

The next expedition set sail on April 9, 1585. In command was Sir Richard Grenville, an experienced sea captain. He was also Walter's first cousin from Devon.

The ships landed at Roanoke Island off the coast of North Carolina. The men set about building houses for themselves. But the 107 settlers had a rough time of it. Food was scarce and the island offered little protection from Spanish ships. The famous sea explorer Sir Francis Drake visited the colony in 1586. The settlers begged him to take them back to England, and he did.

Despite the hardships, Walter continued his push to establish colonies in the New World. The following year, 1587, another expedition sailed for Virginia. Walter had decided that this one would be a permanent

Explorers often took an artist along to draw and paint the previously unknown animals, plants, and native peoples of the region they were going to explore. John White was the artist who sailed with Grenville in 1585 to Roanoke Island. It is believed that many of White's paintings had to be thrown overboard when the colony was later evacuated. Those that did survive give us our best idea of how the New World looked to the eyes of these Elizabethan settlers.

Some people believe that John White the artist is the same John White whom Raleigh appointed governor of the second Roanoke colony in 1587. However, this has never been proven.

This view of a Native American village, based on a painting by John White during the first expedition to Roanoke Island, was meant to provide scientific documentation of the expedition's discoveries.

colony. Women and children sailed with the men. Walter's vision was that each of the 14 families would receive a parcel of land and make their homes there.

The colonists landed on Roanoke Island. They built cabins and planted crops. When the first baby was born, to the Dare family, she was named Virginia.

However, the settlers again faced difficult conditions. The Indians were no longer friendly. The soil wasn't as fertile as they hoped, and they were running out of supplies. The colonists decided to stay put for the winter. In the spring they would move 50 miles north, where the soil was supposed to be more fertile.

Walter received word that the colonists needed supplies. But in the summer of 1588, he was distracted by a crisis brewing at sea. The Spanish **Armada**—Spain's great fleet of 134 warships—was traveling toward London. A panicked Elizabeth sent England's warships out to meet them. With the 30 ships went 50 privately owned ships, including two owned by Walter. Nine thousand sailors were aboard.

Walter had always despised rich and powerful Spain. He begged Elizabeth to let him join the men aboard the ships. But Elizabeth stubbornly refused to let him go. She wanted him on land, in case the Spaniards decided to come ashore.

On the night of July 19, 1588, British lookouts spotted the Spanish Armada on the horizon. The mood was grim. No one expected the quicker English ships to be a match for Spain's powerful Armada.

But before the Spanish realized what was happening, bullets tore into their ships. The quicker English ships darted about in the water. The Spanish didn't know where to aim their guns.

The battle went on for nine days. Walter later wrote about the fight against the Spanish Armada: "Their navy, which they termed invincible, were by 30 of Her Majesty's own ships of war . . . beaten and shuffled together." To everyone's surprise England had stopped the Armada. By the time the Spanish went limping home, their fleet had lost more than 60 ships.

The English navy's strategy of sending eight unmanned fire ships (background) toward the Spanish Armada to scatter and weaken it while it anchored off Calais was successful. The Armada was defeated the next day.

The fight at sea was an incredibly important victory for Sir Walter's country. England had shown her strength and might against a powerful enemy. The English had crippled the strongest fleet in the world.

Elizabeth II at Roanoke Island Festival Park in Manteo, North Carolina. The ship was built to 16th-century specifications and is much like the ships that Raleigh sailed.

3
Keeping Secrets From the Queen

After the Spanish Armada had been defeated, Walter turned back to everyday matters. One thing on his mind was the fate of the colony in the New World. He arranged for a party to return to Roanoke Island with badly needed supplies.

On March 20, 1590, the rescue expedition set sail. No one had heard from the colony in a long time. The men worried that the colonists hadn't survived.

The expedition reached the colony five months later. To their relief, the crew saw smoke rising from

The sandy beaches and scrub pines of the land around Roanoke Island are much the same as when the colonists landed there.

the island. As the men approached, they sounded a trumpet and called out familiar English songs. They wanted the settlers to know that help was on the way. But there was no reply.

In the morning, the group went ashore. They quickly realized that the smoke they'd sighted wasn't from a campfire—it was from a forest fire. Their dread grew as they walked to the site of the settlement.

The settlers' cabins were now surrounded by overgrown weeds. Wooden chests containing their belongings had been torn open. There were only two clues as to where the settlers might have gone: the beginning of a word, "CRO," had been carved into a tree and the word "CROATOAN" had been carved on one of the posts surrounding the fort. The men wondered if this was a signal that the colonists had moved to Croatoan Island.

The rescue party wanted to sail to the island to investigate. Unfortunately, foul weather damaged their ships before they could

Each summer for the past 60 years, the mysterious events that led to the disappearance of the settlers on Roanoke Island are reenacted on the exact location where they took place over 400 years ago. *The Lost Colony,* an outdoor play performed at the island's Waterside Theatre, recreates scenes from Queen Elizabeth's court as well as an Indian raid.

The north end of the island is regularly visited by historians and archaeologists hoping to uncover new evidence about the fate of the lost colony. Recent discoveries have included evidence of Indian occupation and a gold ring dating from the period of English settlement.

leave. Several more dangerous storms prevented the men from traveling further. Finally they had no choice but to return to England. To this day, what happened to the lost colony on Roanoke Island is a mystery.

For Walter, the disappearance of the settlers was a huge disappointment. He had been the main force behind the movement to settle a permanent colony in the Americas. He had used his own money and his influence with the queen. He hoped to send another expedition someday soon.

In the meantime, Walter faced some trouble at home. He was still a favorite of Elizabeth. But a younger man was beginning to compete with him for her attention. His name was Robert Devereux, earl of Essex. Essex was from a noble family and was distantly related to the queen. He was tall and handsome, with blond hair. He acted boldly toward the lonely queen, flattering her with his attentions. The queen had been spending more and more time with him.

Walter and Essex did not get along at all. Walter thought the younger man was vain and simple-minded. Essex was jealous of Walter's sharp mind and talent as a poet. Only Elizabeth could keep the peace between them.

Then, sometime around 1589, Essex made a fateful mistake. He secretly took a wife.

Queen Elizabeth was furious. Marriage was a very sore subject for the queen,

Essex (above) and Walter were bitter rivals. They once planned to fight a duel, but Elizabeth prevented it.

who had never wed. When one of her favorites married, she took it as a personal rejection. She became especially angry when the marriage was done in secret.

Wounded by Essex's behavior, Elizabeth turned back to Walter. Surely *he* would never betray her trust. She rewarded his loyalty by giving him more land. She also gave him an important title: vice-admiral of the fleet.

Meanwhile, Spain was still a threat to England. Spanish explorers had discovered gold and silver in mines in South America. The country grew richer and richer by bringing home vast treasures from the New World.

One day Walter approached the queen. He told her that the most swift way to hurt Spain was to empty its pockets. His idea was to send English ships to patrol the sea approaches to Spain. The English ships could capture the Spanish ships. More importantly, they could also capture their precious **cargo.**

The queen agreed to Walter's plan. In 1591, his **privateering** ships sighted a fleet of ships headed for Spain. Sure enough, the ships were treasure **galleons**—filled with gold and silver.

The Englishmen planned to board the galleons and steal the precious treasure. But something stopped them: the galleons were being escorted by a fleet of Spanish warships!

The privateers quickly turned to flee. Walter's cousin, Richard Grenville, stayed behind. He covered the other men's flight with his ship, the *Revenge.*

A famous sea battle soon began. The Englishmen managed to fight off the Spaniards for 15 hours. But once their ammunition was gone, the Spanish boarded the *Revenge.* Sir Grenville and more than half of his crew were killed.

When the news of the battle reached home, rumors and stories began flying. Walter took it upon himself to write an accurate account of the battle. It was published as a pamphlet and made him well-known throughout England.

The English had been defeated this time. But Walter wasn't ready to give up on his plan to make England rich. He sent more privateering ships. Within a few months, they brought home treasures worth about $200,000.

Elizabeth was very grateful. In 1592, she presented Walter with Sherborne Castle in Dorset.

This beautiful estate was set on many lush green acres and was quite a prize. For the rest of his life, Walter considered it his beloved home.

The queen's generous gift marked the high point of Walter's career. By now he'd become a powerful, wealthy man. He was famous throughout England. But Walter had kept secrets from his queen—secrets that she was about to uncover.

For some time Walter had been courting Elizabeth Throckmorton. "Bess," as she was called, was one of the queen's maids of honor. She was also beautiful and strong-willed. Records show that Walter married her on November 19, 1591. Even though he knew very well what had happened to Essex after his secret marriage, Walter had done the same thing: he'd married Bess in secret.

Walter schemed desperately to keep the news hidden from the queen. But rumors flew all over London. At last, when it was obvious that Bess was expecting a baby, the Queen caught on.

Queen Elizabeth did nothing at first. It was as if she was waiting for Walter and Bess to apolo-

Raleigh's home, Sherborne Castle, was used as a hospital for wounded soldiers during World War I and as a headquarters for the commandos of the D-day landings in World War II. It is open to the public today.

gize. But Walter and Bess were both very proud and stubborn. Instead of begging the queen's forgiveness, they acted as if nothing had happened. Their attitude made the queen even more angry.

Finally, Elizabeth made her move. In August of 1592 the couple was arrested—and imprisoned in the Tower, London's notorious prison.

Walter's first stay in the Tower of London lasted only a month. The Tower was used as a prison for only the most important prisoners. Queen Elizabeth's mother, Anne Boleyn, had also been imprisoned here. Common criminals were never housed in the Tower.

The City
of Gold

Walter's great days as Queen Elizabeth's trusted friend and adviser were over. By marrying Bess, Walter had brought about the beginning of his own downfall. He and Bess were confined to separate cells in the Tower. They were not allowed to see each other. Walter wrote letters to the queen, reminding her of his faithful service to her. He was trying to win their release.

Queen Elizabeth intended to punish the couple for a long time. But only one month later, a situation arose outside of London. The queen needed Walter's help.

The Tower of London is a cluster of grim-looking buildings that sits near the River Thames. The oldest building was built by William the Conqueror in 1078. The rulers after William used it as a fortress, palace, and prison.

All of the buildings in the Tower have thick, stone walls. The cells inside were very dark and damp. Executions and torture were also practiced there. No wonder a sentence in the notorious Tower was feared so much by the people of Walter's time!

Today the Tower serves as a museum. It contains an armor collection, which was started by Henry VIII. It also houses crowns, scepters, and other royal treasures.

His privateering ships had captured the great Spanish galleon, *Madre de Dios*. It had been returning from the East Indies with a huge cargo of rare spices, diamonds, pearls, silk, and gold.

The captured ship was brought into Dartmouth Harbor. By now, word of the ship's valuable treasure had spread. A crowd of fishermen, sailors, jewelers, and merchants stormed the ship. They broke open treasure chests and barrels, eagerly stuffing their pockets. A frenzy of selling and trading broke out on the dock.

News of the looting soon reached the queen. She sent

Dartmouth's deep harbor (pictured here) made it possible for the enormous Spanish galleon *Madre de Dios* to be moored there after its capture.

Sir Robert Cecil to stop the mob from stealing her share of the treasure.

Sir Robert Cecil was the son of Lord Burghley, one of Elizabeth's most trusted advisers. But Sir Robert—a hunchback who stood only five feet tall—was not a very imposing figure. It quickly became clear that he was no match for the unruly mob. He sent a desperate message to the queen: "Only Sir Walter Raleigh can control these wild and willful people. Were he released from prison, he might come here speedily."

Elizabeth rushed an order for Walter's release. He rode swiftly to Dartmouth. The harbor was in Devonshire, the county where he'd been born. When he appeared on the dock, a joyful cheer rose from the crowd.

Sir Robert Cecil watched in amazement as Walter quickly restored order. Best of all, he managed to save some of the treasure for the queen. Although a lot had been stolen, it still took 10 ships to carry the cargo to London. In the end, the queen received half of the wealth. Walter had invested a lot of his own money in the privateering ships. But he himself received almost nothing—except his release from prison.

By the end of 1592, both Walter and Bess were free. However, the queen was not completely through with her punishment. For the next five years, Walter was not permitted at court. Bess was never permitted to return.

Walter and Bess retreated to Sherborne Castle. They quietly set about turning the lovely estate into a home. They planted trees and plants, many of which had been brought back from Virginia and other foreign lands. Walter also surrounded himself with interesting people. A stream of visitors—scientists, writers, philosophers—flowed through the Raleighs' home. They provided Walter with stimulating conversation. They also continued to stir his interest in exploration.

During this time, many people believed a city of gold existed in South America. Stories traveled across Europe about El Dorado, a city of pure gold that was hidden in the jungles above the Orinoco River. According to the legends, the people there bathed in oil, then powdered themselves with gold dust.

As time went on, Walter became more and more intrigued by the legend of El Dorado. He wanted to see this magnificent city for himself. He also secretly hoped that the discovery of riches would put him back in the queen's good graces. He soon began preparing for an expedition to the Orinoco River in the Guiana jungle.

Bess did not want Walter to go. She worried that he would never find the city and would never return to her and their infant son. She wrote to Sir Robert Cecil, asking for his help in discouraging Walter. But Sir Robert, along with some other London men, were eager to make England rich, too. They provided Walter with the ship. Even the queen supported his voyage.

In the spring of 1595, Walter landed in Trinidad, off the coast of South America. He and his men easily captured a Spanish fort. Then they headed south along a channel, which would take them to the river.

The channel was known as "Serpent's Mouth" because it was so narrow and dangerous. Sure enough, it was a difficult trip. The men traveled in open boats. The hot sun was unbearable to the Englishmen, who were not used to the tropical climate. Many of them were ill. One

In 1595 Sir Walter Raleigh captured a fort on Trinidad before returning to sea. He then traveled over 300 miles down the Orinoco River in Guiana to search for the fabled El Dorado.

man was even eaten by a crocodile before their very eyes!

A miserable Walter wrote, "There was never any prison in England that could be found more loathsome." Even he was almost ready to give up.

But then things changed. The land on both sides of the river became green and lush with groves of trees. Indians approached the party with offerings of meat and coconuts. Raleigh and his men quickly befriended them.

The native people showed Walter and the other English explorers many amazing new things—animals such as parakeets and armadillos. They introduced them to the "princess" of fruits, the delicious pineapple. Walter was awed by the beautiful land and sights. He enjoyed meeting the Indians. In fact, they wanted Walter to stay and protect them from Spanish explorers.

Walter was convinced he'd discovered paradise when a blow struck. Heavy tropical rains began to fall. The river rose swiftly, pushing the English boats back. Walter wanted to travel down the river again, but an Indian chief discouraged him. He told Walter to come back another time, bringing more men.

Walter was forced to admit defeat. Unhappily, he gave the order for the expedition to return home.

Walter was very uneasy about returning to England. He and his men had discovered many new things. But they had not discovered any gold. The queen and others who'd invested in the expedition would be upset.

Back at home, Walter was greeted as coldly as he'd feared. Elizabeth made it clear he was still unwelcome at court. His enemies taunted him and spread the news about his failure to find El Dorado, the city of gold.

Once again Raleigh retreated to his home at Sherborne Castle. But he was unable to forget the beautiful land he'd explored. He wrote a book about it, entitled *Discovery of the Large, Rich, and Beautiful Empire of Guiana.*

Walter hoped his description of the lush paradise would spark more interest in exploring the Americas. The book did become a bestseller in England, but it failed to impress the queen. Walter had to wait a long time before he could return to South America.

Essex's attack on Cadiz in 1596 did not cause permanent harm to the city. It continued to flourish and became the official center for trade with the New World.

The New King

Trouble with Spain continued to brew. In the spring of 1596, Queen Elizabeth decided it was time to strike another blow against their old enemy.

Cadiz was Spain's largest and richest port. Elizabeth wanted to attack Cadiz and capture Spain's entire treasure fleet.

The queen named Walter one of the leaders of the attack. That June he sailed for Cadiz, along with 14,000 other men.

Walter's old rival, Essex, was a chief in command. But when Essex made several blunders,

Walter stepped in. Confidently, he led the attack on a mighty Spanish warship. He then ordered the English ships to go ashore and capture the city. During the battle that followed, Walter was shot in the leg. It was an injury that caused him to limp for the rest of his life.

The Spanish were determined to keep the English from seizing their treasure. They set their galleons on fire before the Englishmen could board them.

The soldiers didn't return to England with any great riches. But the event at Cadiz was an important personal victory for Walter. Before, many people had seen him as ambitious and interested only in advancing his own career. By stepping in to save the situation at Cadiz, Walter had displayed his bravery and loyalty to England. Queen Elizabeth was so impressed with the way he'd taken command, he was invited back to court at last in 1597.

Walter was glad to be back in the queen's favor. Once again she seemed to enjoy his company. But another person at court was *not* pleased to see Walter again.

Sir Robert Cecil was still one of the queen's closest advisers. Because of his hunchback and misshapen body, many people called him "Dwarf Cecil." Like Walter, Cecil had a sharp, clever mind. But now that Walter and the queen were friends again, Cecil became extremely jealous of Walter's tall, handsome appearance and his talents as poet, sailor, soldier, and explorer.

While Queen Elizabeth was alive, there wasn't much Cecil could do about Walter. But the queen who had reigned over England for over 40 years was aging. In the winter of 1603 Elizabeth became ill with a cold. On March 24, she died. James VI, king of Scotland, became James I, the new king of England.

Cecil quickly went to work. He flattered the new king and made himself appear indispensable at court. Once he had the king's ear, he told James that Walter was an **atheist.** Knowing that James hated smoking, Cecil told the new king

Elizabeth I's refusal to marry guaranteed that the power of the throne of England remained in her hands while she was alive. She waited until the hours just before her death to name her heir.

James VI of Scotland, the son of Mary Queen of Scots, had a strong claim to the English throne. Elizabeth had kept in close touch by letter during the last years of her life, but even he was not sure whether Elizabeth would decide to name him her successor.

that Walter was the one who had made the habit so popular in England. Cecil also managed to create the false impression that Walter was plotting against the new king.

Little by little, Cecil's plan worked. James stripped Walter of his political powers and confiscated some of his wealth. Then in July 1603, James had Walter arrested for **treason.**

There was a trial and Walter tried to defend himself. But it was no use. James considered Walter a threat. He wanted him in prison. Walter was found guilty and sentenced to die.

When the news of the sentence became public, many people were outraged. How could one of England's brightest and bravest men be charged with treason? James was still a new king. He didn't want to risk making a lot of people angry. Reluctantly, he changed Walter's sentence from death by execution to life imprisonment.

In many ways Cecil and King James had successfully defeated Walter. He'd lost his power and influence, and much of his wealth. But Walter was very stubborn. And now his stubbornness served him well. He was determined to keep his spirit and mind alive. During his dark time in the Tower, his brilliance continued to shine through.

James I's strong opinions about the evils of tobacco, witchcraft, and Puritanism brought him into conflict with many groups of people in England.

Walter had two rooms on the second floor of the prison. He built himself a small laboratory.

Walter Raleigh wrote many books and political and philosophical essays. He is perhaps most famous for his poetry, which was praised by fellow writers. Many of the poems were written to honor Queen Elizabeth. His most passionate love poems were written for his wife, Bess Throckmorton.

As a poet, Raleigh was associated with a group of writers called the "School of Night." Christopher Marlowe and George Chapman were also members. The men discussed many things, including new scientific ideas and mathematics. They also criticized the Bible. This made some people think they were atheists. However, many of Walter's poems, and his final speech before execution, reveal his strong faith in God.

By doing experiments in the lab, he discovered that **quinine** could be used for medicine. He invented a new way to turn salt water into fresh water and a new way to cure tobacco.

Luckily, Walter was not too uncomfortable. Two servants looked after him, and Bess was allowed to visit. She even gave birth to another son, Carew, in 1605.

Another one of Walter's frequent visitors was Prince Henry, the son of King James. Henry was very different from his father. He enjoyed his long conversations with Walter, who knew so much about so many

More than 12 years of Walter's life were spent in the Tower of London. He made good use of the time by writing and studying.

things. As for Walter, the 14-year-old boy bright-ened up his days. It was for Henry that Walter wrote his masterpiece, *A History of the World,*

Beginning with Creation. The book was designed to be a history lesson for Henry, who was expected to one day succeed James as king. It began with the creation of the world. Walter planned to write four parts, taking the reader to the present day.

Walter's friendship with Henry also brought him new hope. Henry tried to persuade his father to release Walter. When Lord Cecil died suddenly in 1612, it seemed as if Henry might succeed. But Walter was dealt another cruel blow. Henry himself suddenly fell ill and died.

When Henry died, the grief-stricken Walter stopped writing his history of the world. He concluded the book at 132 B.C. Its final words are devoted to Henry: "My lyre is changed into the sound of mourning, and my song into the voices of people weeping."

Walter would stay in the Tower for four more years. Finally, a scandal helped one of his friends rise to a position of power. The friend urged Walter to write to the king about his travels to South America, telling about the promise of gold there.

Walter's letter worked. In 1616 James signed the papers for Walter's release so that he could return to Guiana to search for gold. But there was one condition: James wanted to keep peace with Spain. Walter had to promise that no Spaniards would be injured or killed during his expedition. If any *were* injured, James warned ominously, Walter would lose his own life.

Walter agreed. On March 19, 1616, the gates surrounding the Tower were flung open. Bess was joyfully waiting outside in a coach. After 12 long years of imprisonment, Walter was free.

Although Queen Anne and James I lived apart after 1606, James continued to admire her and grieved after her death. She remembered Walter's kindness to her son and tried to influence the king on his behalf.

Walter Bids Farewell

Walter was 63 years old when he was released from the Tower. He was still a tall, handsome man. But now gray flecked his hair and beard. Wrinkles lined his face. He had suffered several strokes while in prison and he was not in good health.

London had changed a lot, too. The city had grown, new buildings had sprouted up all over the city. People, horses, and coaches now crowded the narrow streets. Men and women dressed in unfamiliar fashions. Walter was amazed by everything he saw.

He immediately began preparing for his return to Guiana. He knew it would be hard—maybe even impossible—to avoid conflicts with the Spaniards. But he didn't have a choice. He had to follow the king's orders.

Walter sold some of his things to raise money for the voyage. He borrowed money from others. At last he managed to scrape together enough for seven ships and a crew. His own son was one of the men aboard.

The expedition set sail in August 1617. It was a stormy trip across the ocean. The fleet was forced to stop several times. For four weeks Walter himself was very ill with fever. Forty-two men died along the way. When the fleet finally reached South America, Walter knew he was too weak to survive the difficult trip that still lay ahead. He decided that he would stay with the main fleet while 400 men traveled up the Orinoco River. They planned to head toward a spot where two gold mines were said to exist.

In the meantime, King James was plotting against Walter. The king was laying a trap that Walter and his men would walk right into.

Before the expedition departed, the king had ordered Walter to hand over a list of ships. Walter also had to supply other details about the voyage, such as the ships' route and the type of weapons aboard. James secretly passed along this information to his friend, Count Gondomar.

Gondomar was the Spanish **ambassador** in England. He was also the relative of a man who'd once been captured by Walter. Now Gondomar wanted revenge. Count Gondomar gave the information about Walter's expedition to the king of Spain, Philip III. When Walter's men set out along the river, a group of Spaniards was lying in wait.

For two months, Walter waited off the coast of Trinidad. He spent the time studying medicinal plants, writing in his journal, and worrying about the fate of his men.

Rumors about a skirmish with a group of Spaniards began to drift back to him. Two Englishmen had supposedly been killed. Walter's sense of doom deepened everyday.

On February 14, 1618, Walter received a letter from Lawrence Keymis, the man in charge of the river expedition. The English had battled with the Spanish. Even worse was the news that his son, Wat, had been killed.

Walter was heartsick. He had lost his son—and when he returned to England, he would be executed as well.

The situation only got worse. The men returned to report that they hadn't found the gold mines. Walter lost his temper with Lawrence Keymis. Keymis was so distressed, he went to his cabin and shot himself.

Walter's brave, fierce spirit was broken. He had suffered through many things in his lifetime. But the loss of his son and his friend, along with the failure of the expedition, was too much for him.

Several men tried to convince Walter not to return to England, where he'd face certain execution. They urged him to sail for Virginia and start a new life.

Walter had always longed to see Virginia for himself. But his sense of duty was too strong. He didn't want people to think that he was fleeing from the king's punishment.

Walter's once powerful fleet broke up. Several ships slipped away while others deserted to become pirates. Walter bravely sailed home in his ship, the *Destiny.*

Bess was there to greet him. She, too, begged him to escape from England. Eventually, she managed to convince him.

Walter made a secret plan to escape to France. In the middle of the night his cousin, Lewis Stukely, rowed him out to a ship. The ship would then take him to a French vessel. But Walter didn't know that Stukely had been plotting behind his back. Before they reached the ship, Stukely arrested him.

Walter was stunned by his cousin's betrayal. Stukely was just thinking about the handsome reward he'd receive for Walter's capture.

King James's wife, Queen Anne, remembered Walter's kindness to her son, Henry. She pleaded with her husband to show mercy. Many others pleaded with him, too. But King James had promised Spain that Walter would die. His execution was scheduled for October 29, 1618.

Walter had been sick and he was still very weak. But somehow he managed to summon strength and courage on that dark, cold day. He rose early and inscribed a poem inside his Bible. Then he calmly requested a hearty breakfast, followed by a pipe of tobacco. After his meal, as always, he dressed with great care. He put on a black velvet waistcoat, silk stockings, black taffeta breeches, and an elegant, velvet cloak.

King James knew that Walter had many admirers in England. He had arranged for Walter to be executed on a holiday—Lord Mayor's Day. James hoped that the parades and other

Sir Walter Raleigh is remembered today as a historian, poet, soldier, and adventurer. He was one of the most colorful personalities of the Elizabethan Age.

festivities would keep people away from the execution.

But when Walter walked out of the gate-house, a huge crowd greeted him. Many of his friends had come to pay tribute. Walter's enemies were there, too. They had come to gloat at the fate of the man who'd once been a favorite of Queen Elizabeth.

That morning as Walter climbed the **scaffold,** he held himself with great dignity. He stood so bravely, even his enemies were forced to feel admiration for the gallant statesman.

Walter was given the chance to address the crowd. He spoke for a long time, vigorously declaring that he was being killed just to satisfy Spain. At last it was time to say good-bye, "I have long been a seafaring man, a soldier, and a courtier," he told the crowd. "[Now] I take my leave of you all, making my peace with God."

Then Walter turned to the executioner, who stood holding the ax. "I prithee, let me see it."

After checking to make sure the blade was

sharp, he smiled. "This is a sharp medicine," he joked, "but it is a sure cure for all diseases."

Walter prayed for a minute, then bent over and waited for the ax to strike. But the executioner stood frozen—as if he couldn't bear to end the life of this famous man.

"What dost thou fear?" Walter prodded him. "Strike, man, strike!"

With that, the ax fell. An instant later Walter's head was held up to the crowd. In cases of treason, it was customary for the axeman to declare, "Behold the head of a traitor!"

But this time it wasn't the axeman who spoke. Instead a voice from the crowd shouted, "We have not another such head to cut off!" The person seemed to speak for them all: everyone knew that a great man had lost his life that day.

Sir Walter Raleigh's death made him even more famous throughout Europe. James had to put out a statement explaining why Walter had been executed. Still, the unfair treatment Walter had received stirred people's anger. Many harbored resentment against Spain. After Walter's death Count Gondomar was in danger of being attacked whenever he appeared on the streets of London. And Stukely, the cousin who'd betrayed Walter, was driven out of the country. He went mad and died two years later.

Walter was a brilliant man whose influence has spanned the centuries. As a writer, he created clever poems as well as thoughtful books and essays. As a scientist, he made contributions to the fields of medicine, the study of plants, and geography. A curious man, he longed to see other parts of the world. His interest in exploration made it possible for England to expand her power. It also introduced the people of his home land to different cultures, foods, and ideas.

In many ways Walter Raleigh was ahead of his time. He saw, even as a boy on a Devon beach, the opportunities that lay across the sea.

GLOSSARY

ambassador a person who represents his or her country in a foreign land

armada a group of warships

atheist a person who doesn't believe in God

cargo things carried on a ship

cob-walled walls made of a mixture of clay and straw

colony a group of people living together in a new land and tied by law to their old land

courtier a person who attends a king or queen at court

fleet a group of ships under the same command

galleon a heavy, square-rigged sailing ship used from the 15th to 18th centuries

Huguenots French Protestants

infantry a group of soldiers fighting on foot

monopoly the sole possession or control of something

oracle a person who gives wise opinions

privateering the commissioning of private ships to cruise against an enemy's warships

provisions supplies, such as food

quinine a bitter liquid from bark that is used in medicine

scaffold a raised platform on which prisoners are executed

treason a crime that involves an attempt to overthrow the government

CHRONOLOGY

1552 or 1554 Walter is born at Hayes Barton in Devon, England.

1568 Travels to France to fight for the Huguenot cause.

1578 Leaves England on a voyage of exploration with Sir Humphrey Gilbert.

1580 Travels to Ireland to stop uprisings by Irish rebels.

1581 Appears at Elizabeth's court and becomes a favorite.

1584 Is knighted by the queen, becoming Sir Walter Raleigh; two ships leave for the New World in April; arrive in Carolinas three months later.

1585 Another expedition sets sail for Virginia headed by 107 settlers.

1587 Permanent colony of men and women sails for New World.

1588 England defeats the Spanish Armada.

1590 Rescue expedition returns to the New World and discovers no trace of the colonists on Roanoke Island.

1591 Walter secretly marries Bess Throckmorton.

1592 Queen Elizabeth imprisons Bess and Walter in the Tower.

1595 Walter first travels to Guiana in search of gold.

1596 Leads English attack on Cadiz, Spain.

1597 Invited back to Elizabeth's court.

1603 Queen Elizabeth I dies and James I succeeds her; Walter is arrested for treason and sentenced to the Tower.

1616 Walter is released from prison.

1617 Returns to Guiana.

1618 Returns home to England and is arrested again; executed on October 29.

COLONIAL TIME LINE

1607 Jamestown, Virginia, is settled by the English.

1620 Pilgrims on the *Mayflower* land at Plymouth, Massachusetts.

1623 The Dutch settle New Netherlands, the colony that later becomes New York.

1630 Massachusetts Bay Colony is started.

1634 Maryland is settled as a Roman Catholic colony. Later Maryland becomes a safe place for people with different religious beliefs.

1636 Roger Williams is thrown out of the Massachusetts Bay Colony. He settles Rhode Island, the first colony to give people freedom of religion.

1682 William Penn forms the colony of Pennsylvania.

1688 Pennsylvania Quakers make the first formal protest against slavery.

1692 Trials for witchcraft are held in Salem, Massachusetts.

1712 Slaves revolt in New York. Twenty-one blacks are killed as punishment.

1720 Major smallpox outbreak occurs in Boston. Cotton Mather and some doctors try a new treatment. Many people think the new treatment shouldn't be used.

1754 French and Indian War begins. It ends nine years later.

1761 Benjamin Banneker builds a wooden clock that keeps precise time.

1765 Britain passes the Stamp Act. Violent protests break out in the colonies. The Stamp Act is ended the next year.

1775 The battles of Lexington and Concord begin the American Revolution.

1776 Declaration of Independence is signed.

FURTHER READING

Aronson, Marc. *Sir Walter Ralegh and the Quest for El Dorado*. New York: Houghton Mifflin, 2000.

Buckmaster, Henrietta. *Walter Raleigh: Man of Two Worlds*. New York: Random House, 1964.

Bush, Catherine. *Elizabeth I*. New York: Chelsea House Publishers, 1988.

Campbell, Elizabeth. *The Carving on the Tree*. Little Brown: Boston, 1968.

Syme, Ronald. *Walter Raleigh*. New York: William Morrow and Company, 1962.

Weir, Alison. *The Life of Elizabeth I*. New York: Ballantine Books, 1999.

INDEX

INDEX

PICTURE CREDITS

ABOUT THE AUTHOR

SUSAN KORMAN is a former children's book editor, who currently works as a freelance writer. She is the author of over 15 titles for children, including several series of books. She lives with her husband, three children, and two cats in Bucks County, Pennsylvania.

Senior Consulting Editor **ARTHUR M. SCHLESINGER, JR.** is the leading American historian of our time. He won the Pulitzer Prize for his book *The Age of Jackson* (1945) and again for *A Thousand Days* (1965). This chronicle of the Kennedy Administration also won a National Book Award. He has written many other books including a multi-volume series, *The Age of Roosevelt*. Professor Schlesinger is the Albert Schweitzer Professor of the Humanities at the City University of New York, and has been involved in several other Chelsea House projects, including the REVOLUTIONARY WAR LEADERS biographies on the most prominent figures of early American history.